Yy

**Warren Rylands
and Samantha Nugent**

LET'S READ
AV²
BY WEIGL™
ADDED VALUE • AUDIO VISUAL

AV² provides enriched content that supplements and complements this book. Weigl's AV² books strive to create inspired learning and engage young minds in a total learning experience.

Your AV² Media Enhanced books come alive with...

Go to www.av2books.com, and enter this book's unique code.

BOOK CODE

U 2 2 6 7 6 4

AV² by Weigl brings you media enhanced books that support active learning.

Audio
Listen to sections of the book read aloud.

Video
Watch informative video clips.

Embedded Weblinks
Gain additional information for research.

Try This!
Complete activities and hands-on experiments.

Key Words
Study vocabulary, and complete a matching word activity.

Quizzes
Test your knowledge.

Slide Show
View images and captions, and prepare a presentation.

... and much, much more!

Published by AV² by Weigl
350 5ᵗʰ Avenue, 59ᵗʰ Floor
New York, NY 10118

Website: www.av2books.com

Library of Congress Control Number: 2015940627

ISBN 978-1-4896-3565-5 (hardcover)
ISBN 978-1-4896-3567-9 (single user eBook)
ISBN 978-1-4896-3568-6 (multi-user eBook)

Printed in the United States of America in Brainerd, Minnesota
1 2 3 4 5 6 7 8 9 0   19 18 17 16 15

052015
WEP050815

Project Coordinator: Katie Gillespie   Art Director: Terry Paulhus

Weigl acknowledges Getty Images and iStock as the primary image suppliers for this title.

CONTENTS

2   AV² Book Code

4   Discovering the Letter Y

6   Starting Words with Y

8   Y Inside a Word

10   Ending Words with Y

12   Learning Y Names

14   Different Y Sounds

16   The Y Sound

18   When Y Makes Other Sounds

20   Having Fun with Y

22   Y and the Alphabet

24   Log on to www.av2books.com

Let's explore the letter

The uppercase letter
looks like this

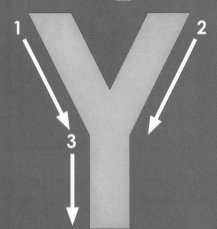

The lowercase letter **y**
looks like this

The letter y can start many words.

yak

yard

yo-yo

yogurt

yes

YES

7

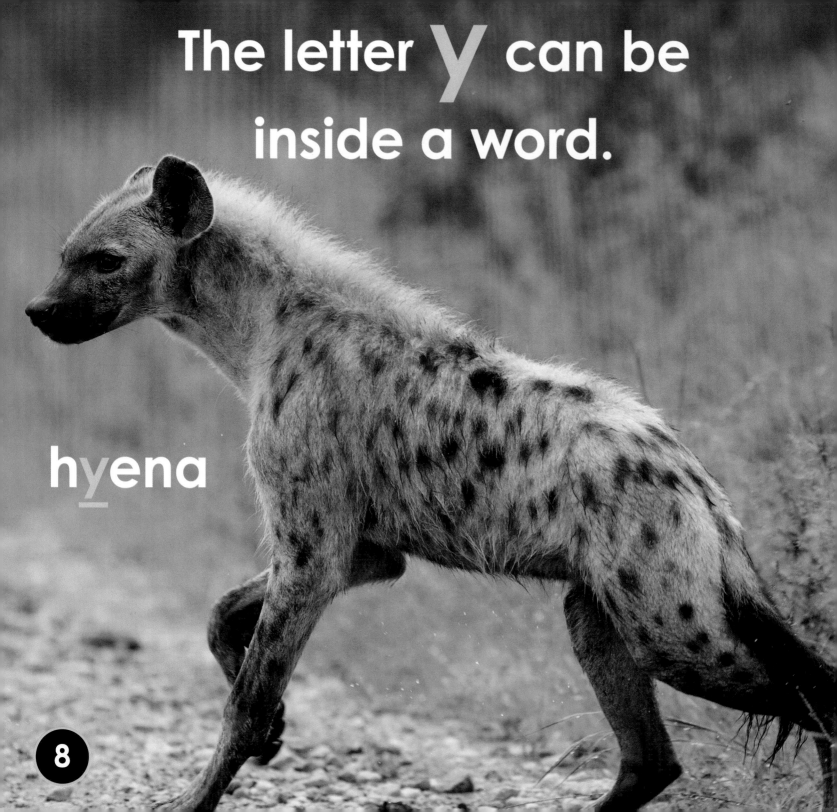

The letter y can be inside a word.

hyena

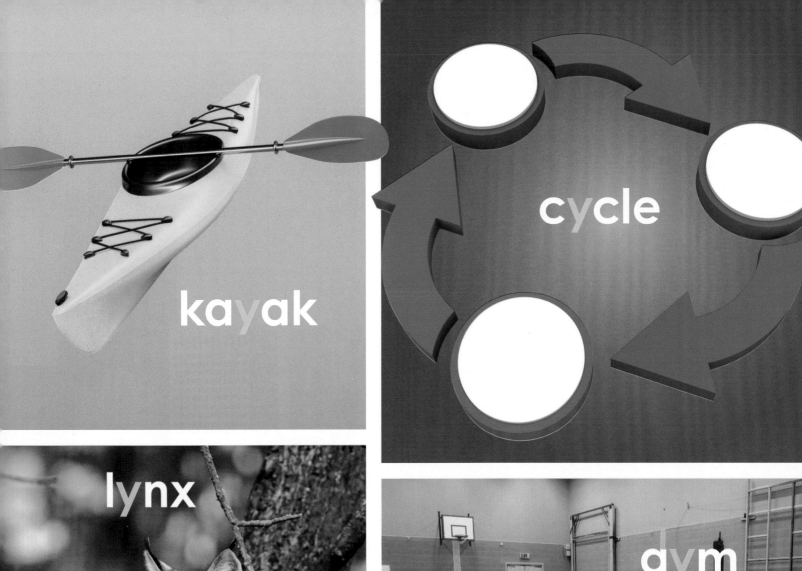

kayak

cycle

lynx

gym

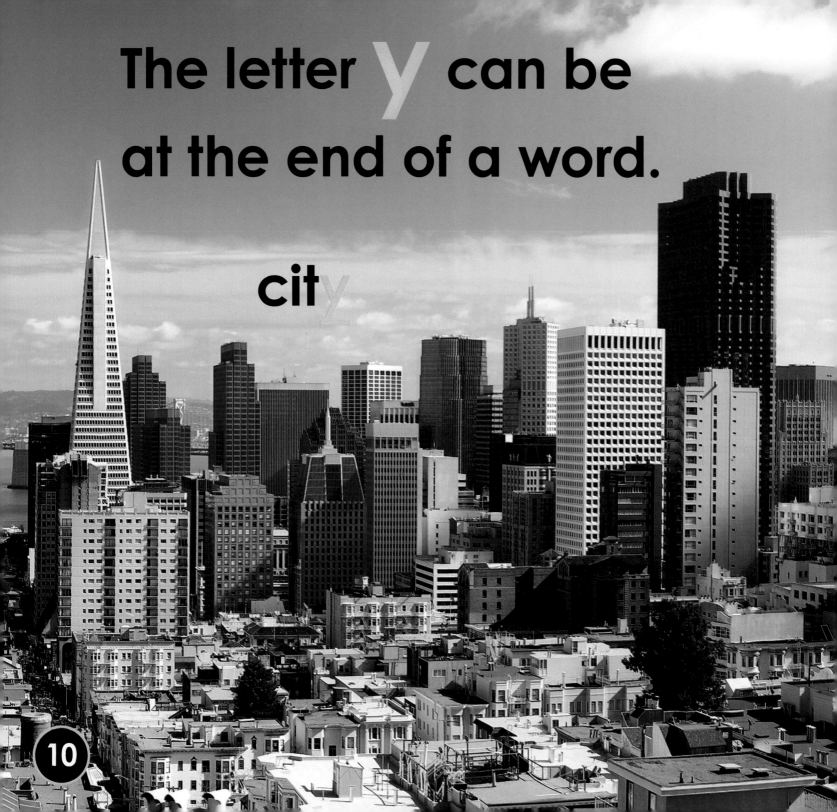

The letter y can be at the end of a word.

city

pony

sky

fly

May

11

Many names start with an uppercase Y.

Yvonne

Yan is loud.

Yolanda can surf.

Yvette loves to talk.

Yale is blue.

The letter **y** makes many sounds.

yam

puppy

The letter y makes the y sound in the word yam.

The letter y makes a long ē sound in the word puppy.

The letter y makes the y sound in many words.

yum

young

years

you

your

17

The letter y can sound
like other letters.

by

baby

symbol

my

many

19

Having Fun with Y

Many young yaks cycle and kayak in May.

In January, they play in the yard.

Yogurt is a yummy snack for young yaks.
Young yaks always say yes to yogurt!

Puppy would rather stay in the yellow house all day.

The alphabet
has 26 letters.

Y is the twenty-fifth
letter in the alphabet.

Aa Bb Cc Dd Ee

Ff Gg Hh Ii Jj Kk

Ll Mm Nn Oo Pp

Qq Rr Ss Tt Uu Vv

Ww Xx Yy Zz

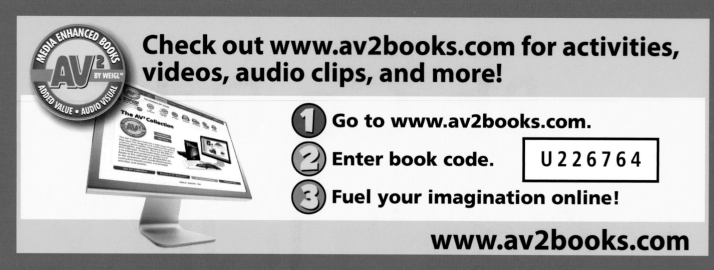

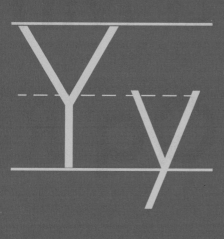